The Cast the Attic

Elizabeth Winthrop

STUDENT PACKET

NOTE:

The trade book edition of the novel used to prepare this guide is found in the Novel Units catalog and on the Novel Units website. Using other editions may have varied page references.

Please note: We have assigned Interest Levels based on our knowledge of the themes and ideas of the books included in the Novel Units sets, however, please assess the appropriateness of this novel or trade book for the age level and maturity of your students prior to reading with them. You know your students best!

ISBN 978-1-56137-830-2

To order, contact your local school supply store, or:

Toll-Free Fax: 877.716.7272
Phone: 888.650.4224
3901 Union Blvd., Suite 155
St. Louis, MO 63115

sales@novelunits.com

novelunits.com

Name_____

 # What Do You Know About Castles?

Directions: After reading each of the following statements, write "True" or "False" in the space provided. If you answer any of the questions incorrectly, do some research to determine the correct answer, and make the corrections as necessary.

1. A European castle was usually thought of as a fortified residence of a feudal lord or monarch. _____

2. The earliest European castle form was the motte and bailey castle. _____

3. The *motte* was the same as the *moat*. _____

4. The open area within the outer walls of the castle was called the *bailey*. _____

5. The accessory buildings of the castle were situated outside of the bailey. _____

6. A castle often had a moat for protection. This was either empty or filled with water. _____

7. A moat was crossed by using a portcullis, which spanned the moat. _____

8. The *motte*, a thick, iron-plated wooden door, could be raised to clear the entrance to the castle. _____

9. Castles in Europe were larger and had more complex designs after the Crusades. _____

10. Eventually, large castles could support town-sized populations. _____

3

Castle Kriss Kross

Directions: This puzzle consists of a list of vocabulary words and a blank puzzle structure. Solve the puzzle by placing the words into the puzzle.

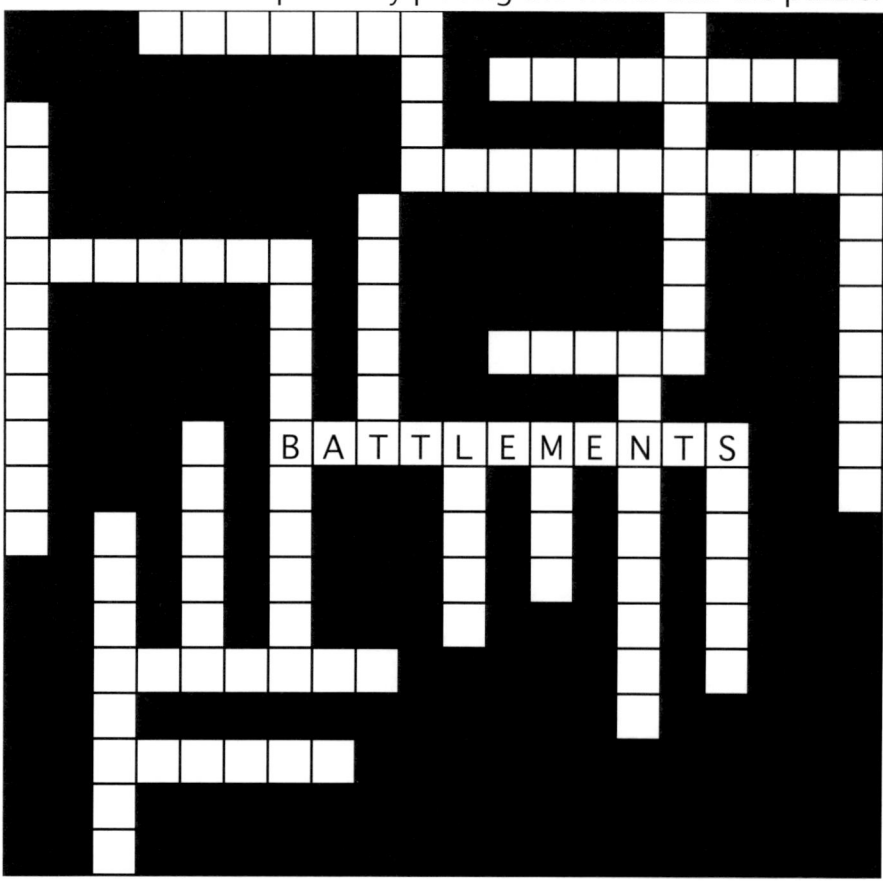

MOAT
SPIT
LISTS
PLUME
ARMORY
KNIGHT
PALLET
SQUIRE
BUTTERY
JESTERS
TANKARD
CHIVALRY
SCABBARD
SCULLERY
WARDROBE
MINSTRELS
DRAWBRIDGE
PORTCULLIS
BATTLEMENTS
TROUBADOURS

Directions: Use as many of the Kriss Kross words as possible in a short written paragraph.

_____

_____

_____

_____

_____

_____

© Novel Units, Inc.

4

Name_____

Study Questions

Write a brief answer to each study question as you read the book at home or in class. Use the questions for review before group discussions and before your final test.

Chapters 1–5 (Pages 3-48)

1. What is the significance of Mrs. Phillips' circle pin and picture of her husband?
2. What does William do with Mrs. Phillips' keepsakes? Why?
3. Why doesn't Mrs. Phillips ask William directly about her missing keepsakes?
4. What is your opinion of the way Mrs. Lawrence handles the inquiry into the missing keepsakes?
5. What do you think Mrs. Phillips means when she says that William has a "gentle heart"?
6. What is the surprise that Mrs. Phillips has for William?
7. What does Mrs. Phillips remember of the legend of the Silver Knight?
8. Why does Mrs. Phillips want to return to England?
9. What is Bear?
10. Why does William take Bear with him to the attic?
11. Why does William drop the knight?
12. What does William learn about the Silver Knight at their first meeting?
13. What words would you use to describe William's relationship with his parents?
14. Why did Jason and William become friends in first grade?
15. Why doesn't William invite Jason to see the castle?
16. What is the knight's story?
17. Why does William offer to bring the Silver Knight a bug?
18. Who is Janus, and why is Janus important to the story?

Chapters 6–9 (Pages 49-92)

19. What does Sir Simon proclaim a miracle in Chapter 6?
20. How does Sir Simon find the word that makes the medallion work?
21. Why do you think William seems uneasy in Chapter 6?
22. What does Mr. Lawrence think of the castle?
23. What does Mr. Lawrence decide to make for the castle?
24. What does Sir Simon do when he encounters a mouse?
25. What fire safety provisions does William make for Sir Simon's cooking?
26. Why is William's gymnastics workout, with Mrs. Phillips in attendance, so successful?
27. Who does William think is the right lady for Sir Simon? What does William plan to do?

28. How does William prevent Mrs. Phillips' departure for England?
29. How does William feel about facing Mrs. Phillips after she is in the castle?
30. How does Mrs. Phillips react to William after he has shrunk her?
31. What changes in routine does Mr. Lawrence propose to William?
32. How does William adjust to his father's trait of being easily distracted?
33. What does Mrs. Phillips want William to do about his own size?
34. What do you think is the meaning of the castle's riddle?
35. Why do you think William wants so desperately to talk with Jason?
36. What important decision does William make about joining Mrs. Phillips?

Chapters 10–13 (Pages 93-139)
37. What about the castle surprises William?
38. How does William learn the rules of chivalry? What rule is added by Mrs. Phillips?
39. How is William's training organized?
40. How will William's training be of help to him?
41. What does Mrs. Phillips believe William will need to defeat the wizard?
42. Why does William declare himself ready to go on his quest?
43. What is "companionable silence"?
44. Why do you think Sir Simon looks sad when he speaks of his horse, Moonlight?
45. What are the "strange apparitions" Sir Simon and William experience in the forest?
46. Who greets William as he leaves the forest?
47. Why do you think William stops to help an old man?
48. How do two birds help William as he descends the tree with the apple?
49. What help does William receive in return for his good deed?
50. How do the villagers react to William as he heads toward Alastor's castle?
51. What decision does William make about facing the dragon that guards the castle?
52. How does William's recorder help him as he faces the dragon?

Chapters 14–17 (Pages 140-179)
53. Where does the "endless spiral of stairs" lead?
54. How is William's first routine for the wizard a success and a failure?
55. What does Calendar have to say about William's dagger?
56. How is William's ability to get past the dragon explained to the wizard?
57. Who are the wizard's pets?
58. Why does William stifle a scream of horror?
59. Why does Calendar befriend William?
60. How does William defeat the wizard?
61. Why does William see so little in the magic mirror?
62. Who determines the fate of Alastor? What is it?

63. Who destroys the mirror and why?
64. How does William restore Sir Simon to life?
65. How are the other leaden people restored to life?
66. What is Calendar's fate?
67. What does William need for Mrs. Phillips?
68. What happens to the wizard's lead medal?
69. What "booty" does Mrs. Phillips show William? What does she do with it? Why?
70. What does Mrs. Phillips take from the castle as a memento?
71. After restoring William to normal size, what will Mrs. Phillips do with the medallion?

Scrambled Words

Vocabulary Words

chivalry (9)	armory (11)	buttery (11)	allure (12)
reckoned (31)	garbled (33)	secretive (34)	mystified (35)

Directions: Unscramble each word. Draw a line to the definition. Include the word in a sentence.

Scrambled Words	Unscrambled Words	Definitions
1. l e a l r u	_____	a. pantry
2. e b l g d r a	_____	b. mixed-up
3. v y h l c i a r	_____	c. bewildered
4. f d i i y e m s t	_____	d. gallantry
5. m y r r o a	_____	e. wall walk
6. k d r e e o c n	_____	f. uncommunicative
7. v i t e e e s c r	_____	g. arsenal
8. t y u e r b t	_____	h. dealt

Sentences:

1. _____

2. _____

3. _____

4. _____

5. _____

6. _____

7. _____

8. _____

Vocabulary—Synonym or Antonym?

secretive (34)	mystified (35)	rummaged (46)	squeamish (52)
meddle (63)	resigned (74)	distracted (76)	inevitable (78)
hasty (80)	desperately (81)	lame (83)	deteriorating (83)

Directions: Match the synonym or antonym in the comparison with a listed vocabulary word.

Sample: GOOD is to BAD as BETTER is to WORSE.

1. MISERY is to HAPPINESS as _____ is to COMMUNICATIVE.

2. COAXED is to PERSUADED as _____ is to DEGENERATING.

3. SULKED is to POUTED as _____ is to RECONCILED.

4. COMPLIANT is to DEFIANT as _____ is to AVOIDABLE.

5. CONTEMPT is to DISDAIN as _____ is to BEWILDERED.

6. CONFRONT is to AVOID as _____ is to PATIENT.

7. DUBIOUS is to DOUBTFUL as _____ is to SIDETRACKED.

8. ADVANTAGEOUS is to FAVORABLE as _____ is to BADLY.

9. SHODDY is to INFERIOR as _____ is to INTERFERE.

10. RELUCTANT is to EAGER as _____ is to STRONG.

11. APPREHENSION is to ANXIETY as _____ is to SEARCHED.

12. INSULT is to COMPLIMENT as _____ is to TOUGH.

Word Find

Directions: Find the words *ale, drafty, earnest, tankard,* and *yellow* hidden in the puzzle below. Begin at "start" and draw a path to find the words. The last letter of one word is the first letter of the next word. After you have completed the puzzle given, make your own Word Find, using different words. The words must use the exact number of spaces provided. Trade Word Finds with a partner.

Words to find: ale   drafty   earnest   tankard   yellow

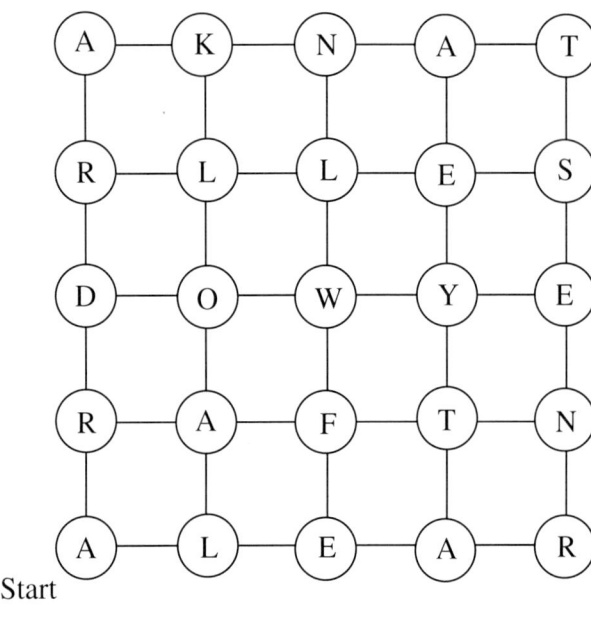

Start

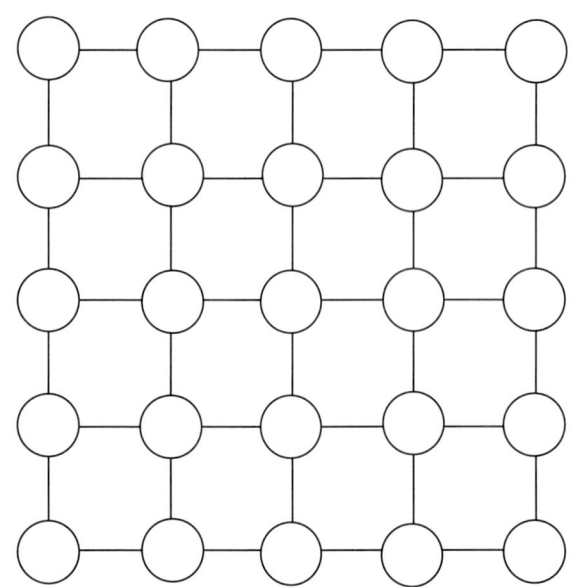

Vocabulary

medallion (51)   armory (53)   unobstructed (59)   allotted (63)
distracted (76)   quest (80)   lame (83)   sheepishly (86)
legacy (86)   contraption (87)   intricate (91)   earnest (97)
incantation (97-98) midday (99)   wanes (99)   firescreen (103)

Directions: Write the vocabulary word that matches each definition or synonym.

1. _____ unrestricted, unblocked

2. _____ sidetracked, thrown off

3. _____ insufficient, poor

4. _____ complicated, complex

5. _____ military building, weapon storage

6. _____ assigned, allocated

7. _____ inheritance, heritage

8. _____ search, hunt

9. _____ device, gadget

10. _____ self-consciously, shyly

RE + [🚌] = **REBUS**

Vocabulary Words Used For This Activity:

drawbridge (10)   armory (11)   buttery (11)   scullery (11)   wardrobe (12)

Directions: Use the letters and the pictures to figure out the words.

1. [🖐️] + [🥄 - A] + Y   = _____

2. [👂😠 - T] + D + [🧥]   = _____

3. [🧈MOO] + Y   = _____

4. [🎨👨‍🎨] + [🌉]   = _____

5. [💀 (K=C)] + [👂 -A] + Y = _____

Make your own REBUS.

Vocabulary

courageous (93)	intricately (94)	earnest (97)	chided (108)
raucous (110)	striding (121)	compassionate (122)	hoisted (123)
stagnant (124)	suffice (127)	haggard (128)	prowled (133)
tumult (136)	anguished (136)	grotesque (138)	matted (141)

Directions: Make a special word map for <u>five</u> of the above vocabulary words. Before following the word map pattern given below, turn to the pages in the book on which each word appears. Look at how each word is used in the story.

Synonyms (words with the same meaning)	Magazine Cutout or Your Sketch to Show What the Word Means
_____ _____ _____ _____	

Word

_____

Definition in Your Own Words	Word Used in a Sentence
_____ _____ _____ _____	_____ _____ _____ _____

Vocabulary Word Search

Directions: Do the word search. Find the words that may be printed forwards, backwards, and on a diagonal. Write down the letters that have not been used, starting at the top and working left to right in each row. Group the letters into words to find the hidden message. (X = a period)

E	D	K	Y	G	P	U	R	S	E	D	W	I	L	L	E	G	T	I	C	N
D	T	E	I	T	N	N	O	T	C	H	A	M	M	D	A	N	U	H	O	D
I	E	A	T	N	F	A	R	O	O	K	S	S	I	R	A	D	I	I	E	D
N	T	N	C	T	D	A	W	T	D	E	S	C	B	R	E	S	L	N	E	U
C	D	S	G	I	O	L	R	E	T	R	T	L	R	T	E	L	O	G	A	O
A	H	E	E	I	R	L	I	D	D	S	E	U	E	L	A	K	A	E	M	R
N	A	P	M	N	S	T	L	N	U	D	C	R	E	D	C	M	R	Q	O	E
T	S	L	Y	O	R	E	N	A	G	N	I	D	E	E	M	U	A	U	U	E
A	T	U	L	A	O	A	R	I	Y	O	O	M	R	U	B	S	T	E	N	L
T	Y	M	E	O	R	L	E	H	R	N	D	B	R	T	T	O	S	S	T	E
I	A	E	L	V	Y	E	P	A	O	E	R	E	S	H	A	S	I	T	R	L
O	S	I	A	C	S	A	T	I	E	Y	S	E	T	T	O	N	M	O	N	D
N	A	N	A	N	R	I	T	L	L	E	M	D	P	C	R	I	K	D	H	D
I	S	G	E	G	N	P	B	H	V	V	S	Y	R	E	A	U	S	A	K	E
I	E	C	O	G	A	A	S	I	A	N	N	C	S	A	R	R	C	T	R	M
L	N	P	G	R	T	I	T	U	D	O	M	O	R	T	U	T	T	T	E	D
I	O	A	T	I	P	E	L	N	E	M	A	L	S	O	I	G	O	S	E	D
T	D	N	V	E	R	T	L	A	Y	S	L	A	P	I	U	F	N	I	I	D
D	O	E	E	C	E	B	R	U	N	T	Y	E	L	I	N	N	I	I	R	D
C	N	H	E	D	N	O	H	S	I	M	A	E	U	Q	S	E	G	E	H	E
I	S	S	D	E	S	P	E	R	A	T	E	L	Y	R	E	X	V	E	D	S

ale	drafty	intricate	notch	scrounge
allotted	earnest	kindling	palsy	secretive
brunt	edicts	lame	plume	sheepishly
bureau	garbled	leer	pursed	shinguards
chiseled	gnawed	legacy	quest	squeamish
contraption	hasty	loomed	reckoned	tankard
currant	hoisted	medallion	repertoire	topography
desperately	incantation	meddle	resigned	unobstructed
deteriorating	incense	mount	rooks	vaulted
distracted	inevitable	mystified	rummaged	venison

Vocabulary

chivalry (9)	scullery (11)	wardrobe (12)	gnawed (17)
mystified (35)	portcullis (56)	unobstructed (59)	withered (133)
falter (136)	ramparts (139)	crone (146)	booty (173)

Directions: Find the missing word for each clue. Write the letters of the word in the space above the numbers. Then transfer the numbered letters to the numbered spaces at the end of the activity. Find out what Mrs. Phillips has to tell William. (page 68)

Definition Clue

1. bewildered   __ __ __ __ __ __ __ __
                 40   14 18 17 43

2. a rich gain or prize   __ __ __ __ __
              31 33

3. iron grating   __ __ __ __ __ __ __ __ __ __
            9   24 13 16 41

4. a withered old woman   __ __ __ __ __
               45

5. kitchen   __ __ __ __ __ __ __ __
      25 22 3 6 7 11   32

6. unrestricted   __ __ __ __ __ __ __ __ __ __ __ __
       34 39 27   19

7. nagged, pestered   __ __ __ __ __ __
         15   10   8

8. stumble   __ __ __ __ __ __
      28   26 46

9. gallantry, valor   __ __ __ __ __ __
                        30 5   23 12 36 1

10. shriveled   __ __ __ __ __ __
                        29 38   44 37   47

11. furniture for clothes   __ __ __ __ __ __ __
    storage   4 35   42   2 20 21

"

__ __ __ __ __ __ __ __ __ __ __ __ __
1 2 3   4 5 6 7   8 9   10 11 12 13

__ __ __ __ __ __ __ __ __ __ __ __ __
14 15 16 17 18 19 20 21 22 23 24 25 26

__ __ __ __ __ __ __ __ __ __ __
27 28 29 30 31 32 33 34 35 36 37

"

__ __ __ __ __ __ __ __ __ __
38 39 40 41 42 43 44 45 46 47

Vocabulary Crossword Puzzle

Directions: Use the clues to figure out the answers to the crossword.

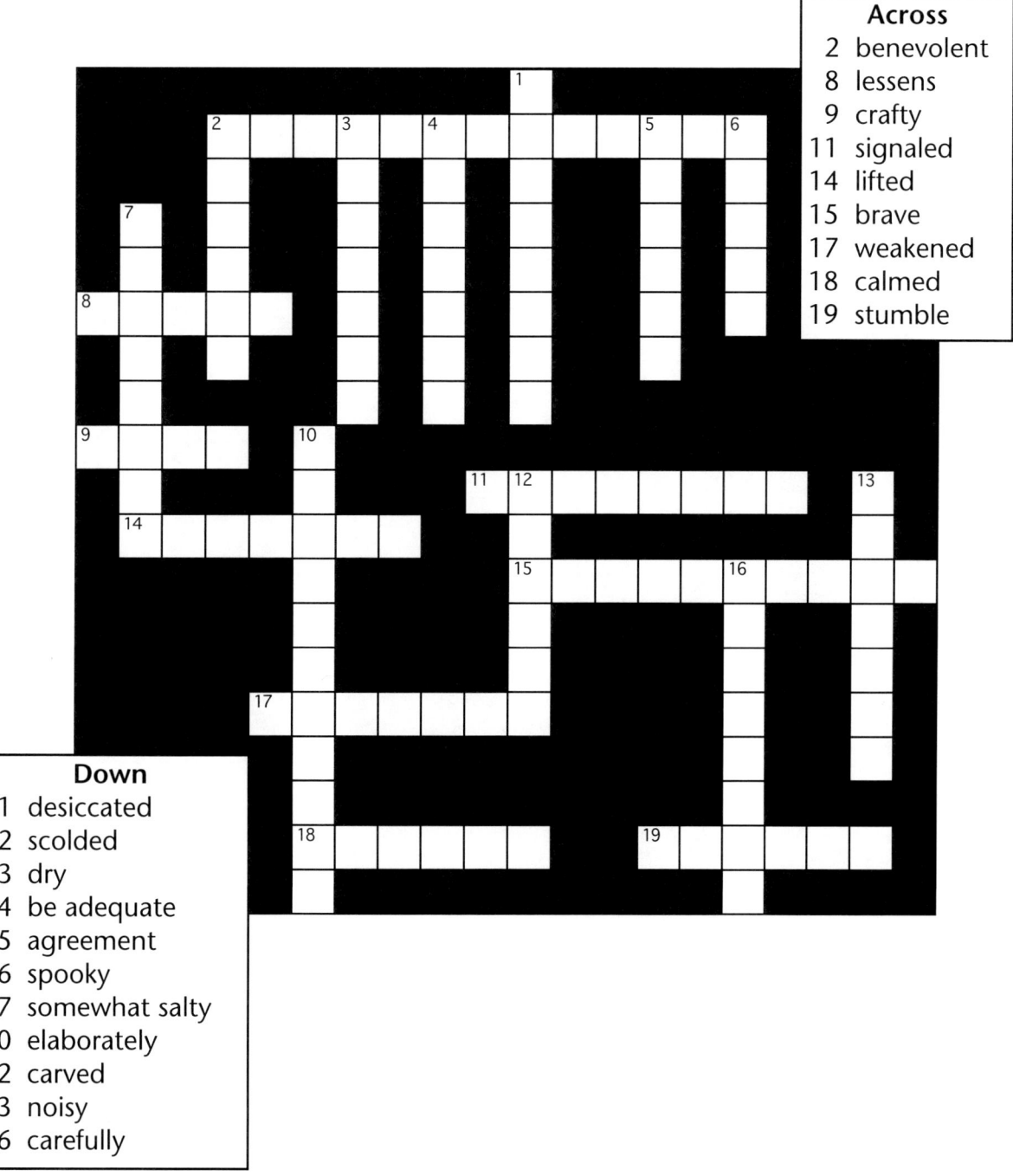

Across
2 benevolent
8 lessens
9 crafty
11 signaled
14 lifted
15 brave
17 weakened
18 calmed
19 stumble

Down
1 desiccated
2 scolded
3 dry
4 be adequate
5 agreement
6 spooky
7 somewhat salty
10 elaborately
12 carved
13 noisy
16 carefully

Phrase It

armory (11)   allure (12)   brunt (28)   palsy (35)
edicts (36)   ale (51)   leer (51)   spit (55)
wok (76)   hasty (80)   quest (80)   lame (83)
notch (85)   legacy (86)   tunic (96)   wanes (99)

Directions: Devise a phrase consisting of words beginning with the letters of at least <u>six</u> of the words listed above. An example follows:

Word Chosen   **Phrase**

Allure   **A**llison **l**icked **l**ollipops **u**ntil **r**ecent **e**vents.

_____

_____

_____

_____

_____

_____

_____

_____

_____

Synonym Chains

assent (132)	prowled (133)	withered (133)	tumult (136)
anguished (136)	falter (136)	grotesque (138)	acrid (141)
beckoned (141)	matted (141)	wily (145)	bide (146)
churlish (151)	scoundrel (151)	agonies (152)	ravager (159)
wizened (163)	gingerly (164)	lulled (167)	eerie (177)

Directions: The object of this activity is to make a chain of synonyms leading from one chosen vocabulary word to a different word altogether, that is not a synonym of the first word. Choose a vocabulary word from those listed above. Think of a synonym for that word and write it next to the vocabulary words. Next write down a synonym of the synonym. Continue on, giving a synonym for the synonym until you no longer have a synonym for the vocabulary word. Make at least <u>eight</u> synonym chains. Use a dictionary and/or a thesaurus if necessary.

Example: scoundrel - villain - cur - cad - boor - yokel - bumpkin - farmer

_____

_____

_____

_____

_____

_____

_____

_____

Alphapat

Vocabulary

bureau	chivalry	entrusted	drawbridge
portcullis	armory	buttery	scullery
troubadours	jesters	minstrels	wardrobe
allure	gnawed	loomed	scabbard
scrounge	topography	brunt	reckoned
battlements	garbled	mystified	palsy
edicts	vaulted	venison	squeamish
unobstructed	pursed	repertoire	wok
quest	kindling	wanes	cacklings
prowled	anguished	grotesque	wily
gyrations	ravager	tyranny	wizened

Directions: Use up all of the letters of the alphabet in building a pattern like a crossword with the vocabulary words. (**X** is eliminated for this activity.) Cross off the letters as you use them. Trade with a partner. Check one another's pattern and letter use. An example follows.

A B C D E F G H I J K L M N O P Q R S T U V W Y Z

Example crossword grid:

```
E           J
D R A W B R I D G E
I     I       S Q U E A M I S H
C     Z       T
T     E       E
S     N       R
      E     M Y S T I F I E D
      D       O
              P
              O
      C A C K L I N G S
              R
              A
              P
              H
      C H I V A L R Y
```

A B C D E F G H I J K L M N O P Q R S T U V W Y Z

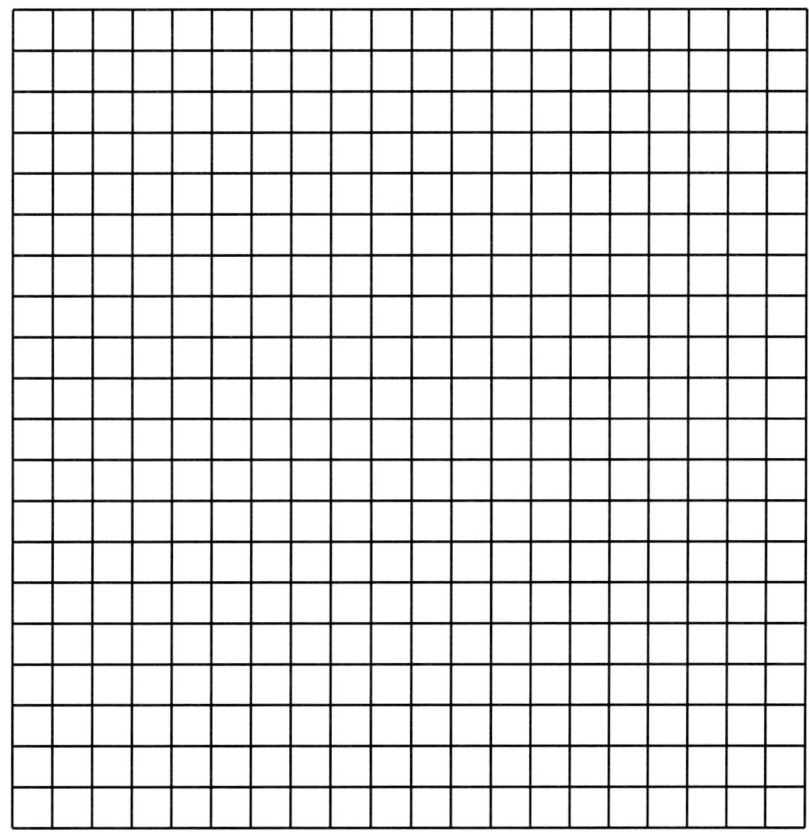

Directions: Define each of your Alphapat words.

_____

_____

_____

_____

_____

_____

_____

_____

_____

Vocabulary Review

bureau (6)	chivalry (9)	wardrobe (12)	reckoned (31)
quest (80)	hoisted (93)	firescreen (103)	drafty (104)
raucous (110)	suffice (127)	battlements (132)	falter (136)
wily (145)	booty (173)	cooped (175)	eerie (177)

Directions: Complete each statement with a word from the box above.

1. William decides that the time is right for a __ __ __ __ __.
   19   3

2. William wakes to the __ __ __ __ __ __ __ call of rooks.
   12 13 38   22   27

3. William does not want to __ __ __ __ __ __ in his quest to find Alastor.
   43 33

4. Mrs. Phillips is __ __ __ __ __ __ up in the castle.
   30 31

5. Mrs. Phillips is working on a __ __ __ __ __ __ __ __ __ __.
   11   14

6. Sir Simon needs company in the __ __ __ __ __ __ old castle.
   21 39 26   36

7. One of the lead people is a __ __ __ __ priest.
   4   16 17

8. William has an __ __ __ __ __ feeling as he looks at the lead people.
41 5 6   9

9. Soldiers patrol the upper __ __ __ __ __ __ __ __ __ __ __ of Alastor's castle.
1 7 20 42   32   34 25 40

10. William's __ __ __ __ __ is the miniature lead wizard.
18 37 24 29 35

Directions: Notice the numbers under some of the letters you have written. Place the correct letter with its matching number on each line below to read one of the rules of chivalry, given on page 98.

"If questions are asked of you,

___ N ___ ___ ___ ___   ___ H ___ M
1   2   3   4   5   6   7   8   9   10

___ ___ ___ ___ K ___ ___   ___ ___ ___   ___ ___ N ___ ___
11 12 13 14 15 16 17   18 19 20   21 22 23 24 25

___ ___ K ___ ___ ___   ___ ___ ___ ___
26 27 28 29 30 31   32 33 34 35

"

___ ___ ___ ___ ___ ___ ___ ___
36 37 38 39 40 41 42 43

Directions: Write your interpretation of this rule of chivalry here:

_____

_____

_____

_____

Cryptogram

Directions: Decode the following to find out what Brian tells William about Alastor. (page 152)

Instructions For Cryptogram Decoding: For the following cryptogram, you will need to discover the code used to encrypt the quote. Use the hints given to determine the code, and then use the code to decipher the quote. Fill in the letter above the line that corresponds to the code representation below the line.

Hint: C = F, A = H, and W = L

"
                     ,

O T H E R   P E O P L E ' S   A G O N I E S   A R E   T H E   O N L Y
"TOADQ   SDTSWD'P   HBTUZDP   HQD   OAD   TUWJ

P L E A S U R E   A L A S T O R   T A K E S   F R O M   L I F E."
SWDHPNQD   HWHPOTQ   OHXDP   CQTV   WZCD"

A	B	C	D	E	F	G	H	I	J	K	L	M
H	G	F	E	D	C	B	A	Z	Y	X	W	V

N	O	P	Q	R	S	T	U	V	W	X	Y	Z
U	T	S	R	Q	P	O	N	M	L	K	J	I

Use a different quote. Encode it with your own cryptogram code. Trade with a partner.

Name_____

The Castle In The Attic
Activity #17: Story Review

Story Review

Directions: Answer each question by circling the letter in the YES or NO column.

		YES	NO
1.	Is William a knight?	B	A
2.	Is Mrs. Phillips William's mother?	Z	E
3.	Is William's father a medical doctor?	W	R
4.	Does Mrs. Lawrence want to return to England?	D	V
5.	Does Mrs. Phillips give William the castle in the attic?	C	X
6.	Is William a gymnast?	U	N
7.	Does Mrs. Phillips like Marmite?	H	J
8.	Is Sir Simon the Silver Knight?	S	K
9.	Does Mrs. Phillips give her consent to live in the castle?	G	I
10.	Is Alastor a wizard?	Y	P
11.	Does William's touch bring the knight to life?	L	Q
12.	Does the wizard reduce William in size?	A	O
13.	Does Alastor turn Sir Simon into lead?	M	S
14.	Does Calendar tell an important secret to William?	F	M
15.	Does Mrs. Lawrence find out about the castle's secrets?	I	T

Directions: Fill in the circled letters that correspond to the numbered questions to find out what William is told he must do to defeat the wizard. (page 154)

— — —   — — —   — — — —   — —   — — — —   — — — — —   — — —
1 11 11   10 12 6   7 1 4 2   15 12   14 1 5 2   9 8   15 7 2

— — — — — —
13 9 3 3 12 3

Story Review Crossword Puzzle

Directions: Use the clues to figure out the answers to the crossword.

Across

1 William's last name
5 Mr. Lawrence's occupation
7 Name of Sir Simon's horse
9 Nanny's last name
10 Name of wizard
13 Place where the castle is kept
15 Mrs. Phillips' memento of the adventure
18 What William must look into to defeat the wizard
19 Creature guarding Alastor's castle
20 First name of William's best friend

Down

2 First name of William's coach
3 Kind of routine William practices
4 First name of the boy who has the castle
6 Mrs. Lawrence's occupation
8 One of Mrs. Phillips' keepsakes
11 Name of knight (2 words)
12 The word January comes from this name
14 She was Sir Simon's old nurse
16 Color of the knight
17 Name of William's stuffed animal
18 What Mr. Lawrence makes for the castle

Similes

Directions: At times authors use figurative language to make descriptions more vivid for readers. **Similes** are comparisons using the words *as* or *like* to highlight the comparison. For example, *She is as happy as a lark.*

Below are some similes used by Elizabeth Winthrop in *The Castle In The Attic*. Analyze each simile by telling what two things are being compared, and how they are alike.

1. "You [William] look like a horse at the starting gate," she said with a laugh. (page 8)

   _____ is like _____ because

   _____.

2. "He [Alfred] would attack one problem over and over again like a baby butting its head against the side of its crib." (page 173)

   _____ is like _____ because

   _____.

3. "By the time she saw the small flames, it was too late, and he had to watch her beating at them with her hands, trying to shield her face as they climbed like living snakes up her tunic." (page 137)

   _____ is like _____ because

   _____.

4. "Spiders had stretched their webs on the bushes, and drops of water glistened on the strands like tears." (page 108)

   _____ is like _____ because

   _____.

Directions: Write three of your own similes on the back of this paper. Explain the comparisons.

Quatrain Poetry

A **quatrain** is a poem written in four lines. It may be rhymed or unrhymed. When the poem rhymes, it may have a variety of rhyming patterns. It is up to the author to decide on the rhyme pattern.

Directions: Write a quatrain poem about one of the characters or situations in the story of *The Castle In The Attic*. Make an illustration for your poem.

_____

_____

_____

_____

True—False Comprehension Quiz

Directions: Label each statement "T" for True or "F" for False. Correct all false statements.

_____ 1.   William is a gymnast.

_____ 2.   Mrs. Lawrence is William's nanny.

_____ 3.   Mrs. Phillips is going to return to England.

_____ 4.   Mrs. Phillips' keepsakes are a circle pin and a photograph of her late husband.

_____ 5.   Mr. Lawrence is a physician.

_____ 6.   Mrs. Phillips gives William the castle in the attic.

_____ 7.   Mrs. Phillips thinks that William is the "right person" for the castle.

_____ 8.   The Silver Knight comes to life when Mrs. Phillips touches him.

_____ 9.   The Silver Knight is Sir Simon of Hargrave.

_____ 10.   Mr. Lawrence makes a tower for the castle.

_____ 11.   William thinks Mrs. Phillips is the right lady for the castle.

_____ 12.   Sir Simon decides to shrink William.

_____ 13.   William learns the rules of chivalry from Sir Simon and Mrs. Phillips.

_____ 14.   Sir Simon leaves the path for his horse, Darkness.

_____ 15.   William's music helps him defeat the dragon.

© Novel Units, Inc.

29

Short Answer Comprehension Quiz

Directions: Answer each question in one complete sentence.

1. What does William do with Mrs. Phillips' keepsakes? Why?

2. What is the surprise that Mrs. Phillips has for William?

3. Who is the Silver Knight?

4. How does the Silver Knight come to life?

5. What does Mr. Lawrence make for the castle?

6. Why doesn't Mrs. Phillips return to England?

7. How does William change in size?

8. Why does William want to fit into the castle?

9. How does William learn the rules of chivalry?

10. What does William do to get ready for his quest?

11. Why does Sir Simon leave the path in the forest?

12. What does William get from the top of the tree for the old man?

13. What help does William receive in return for helping the old man?

14. What decision does William make about facing Alastor's dragon?

15. How does William's music help him defeat the dragon?

© Novel Units, Inc.

30

Identification By Clues

Directions: Find a character on the right who matches the description on the left. Write the letter of the character next to the matching number. Each character is to be used only once.

_____ 1.	He brings the Silver Knight to life.	a. Calendar
_____ 2.	He makes a moat for the castle.	b. Brian
_____ 3.	She is a physician.	c. Mr. Lawrence
_____ 4.	He is the Silver Knight.	d. Alastor
_____ 5.	She is the Silver Knight's nurse/nanny.	e. Robert
_____ 6.	He is William's gymnastics coach.	f. Tolliver
_____ 7.	He has been William's friend since first grade.	g. Sir Simon
		h. William
_____ 8.	He is a wizard.	i. Jason
_____ 9.	He is Calendar's grandson.	j. Mrs. Lawrence
_____ 10.	He guards William in Alastor's castle.	

Directions: Choose one of the characters. Write a description of that character.

_____

_____

_____

_____

_____

_____

Identification By Quotation

Directions: Find a character on the right who matches the quote on the left. Write the letter of the character next to the matching number. Each character is to be used only once.

_____ 1. "I thought it would make you stay." (page 7)

_____ 2. "I know that you are the right person for it." (page 9)

_____ 3. "I am not frightened by your size, my good sir…" (page 21)

_____ 4. "You're lucky. My parents never ask me anything." (page 28)

_____ 5. "The moat. It needs a moat." (page 56)

_____ 6. "William, we will start with your routine." (page 60)

_____ 7. "We shall keep the dagger for you, young Muggins." (page 144)

_____ 8. "I had to watch it happening to him for a second time." (page 153)

_____ 9. "Where's Bear? He's usually in on these conversations." (page 89)

_____ 10. "He divides us so that each is rewarded if he carries tales of another." (page 150)

a. Sir Simon

b. Mr. Lawrence

c. Alastor

d. Mrs. Lawrence

e. Robert

f. William

g. Brian

h. Jason

i. Calendar

j. Mrs. Phillips

Directions: Choose one of the characters. On the back of this paper, write a description of that person.

Fill-Ins

Directions: Fill in each blank with a word or phrase.

This story is about a boy named 1. _____. He is given a 2. _____

by his 3. _____ because she is going back to 4. _____.

There is one 5. _____ , the 6. _____ Knight, to go with

the castle. William brings the knight to life by 7. _____ him. William

uses the token to shrink 8. _____ . 9. Sir _____ uses the token

to shrink 10. _____ so that William can help Mrs. Phillips. Sir Simon

and Mrs. Phillips teach William the rules of 11._____ . Sir Simon and

William follow the 12._____ written on the castle to defeat the wizard,

13. _____ . While going through the forest, 14. _____

is lured off the path by an apparition of his horse, 15. _____ .

After leaving the forest, 16. _____ stops to help an 17. _____

man by getting an 18. _____ for him from the top of the tree. In turn,

William is told how to tame the 19. _____ guarding 20. _____

castle. William gets into the castle, and becomes Alastor's 21._____ ,

Muggins. Sir Simon's nurse/nanny, 22. _____, tells William that he

will have to face the 23._____ to defeat the wizard. William sees only

two things, 24. _____ and 25._____ . The

wizard is defeated, and shrunk into a lead figure by 26. _____ .

Written Response

Directions: Think of words and phrases that describe William, and put them under his name. Then think of words and phrases that tell how William feels about the other characters and how each of them feels about him. Label the arrows with these words and phrases.

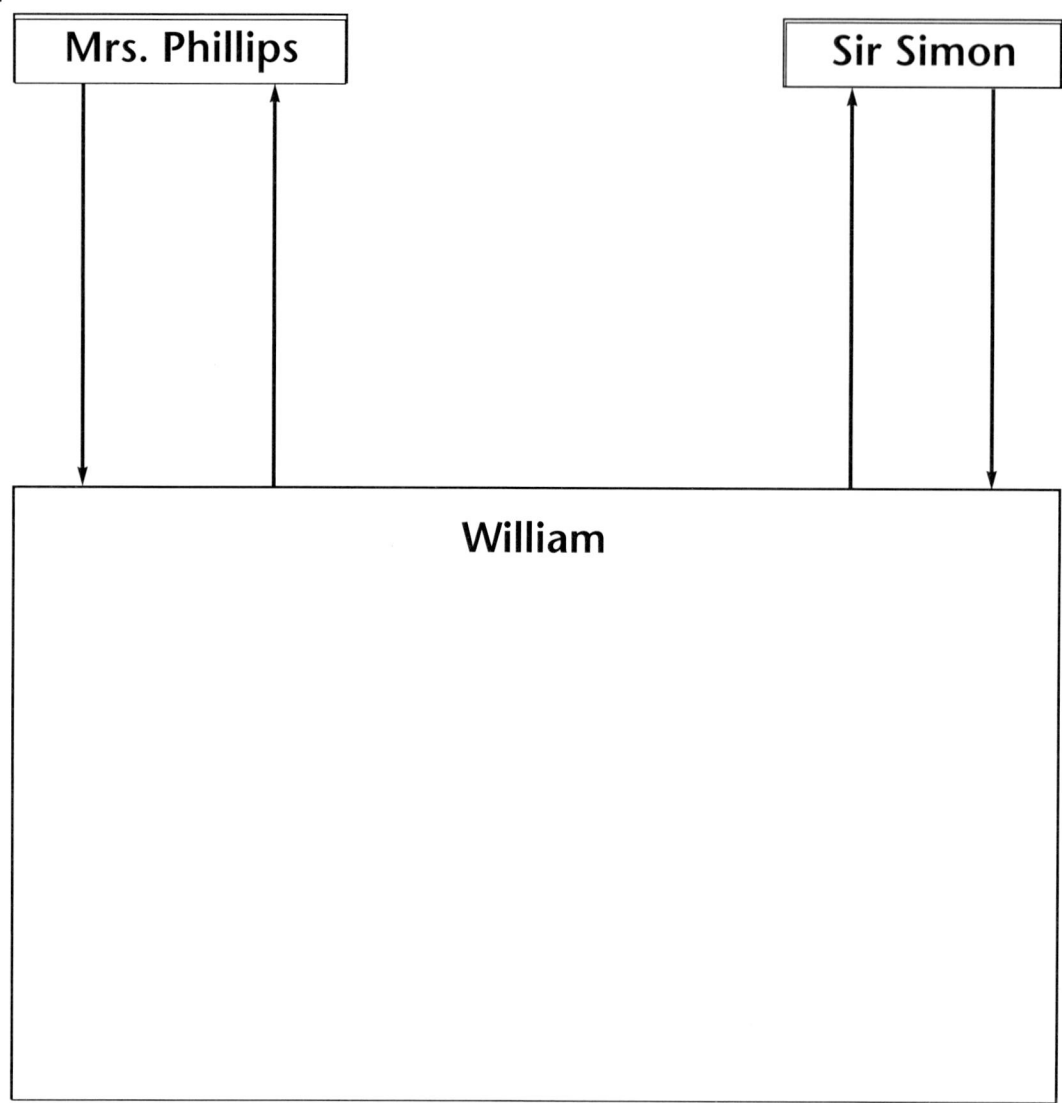

Directions: Using the notes you have written on the chart above, write a character sketch of William. (A **character sketch** is a brief, vivid description of a person. It includes physical characteristics and personality characteristics.)

Multiple Choice

Directions: To the left of each number, write the letter of the BEST response to the question.

_____ 1. What does Mrs. Phillips give to William?
  A. train set
  B. castle
  C. bicycle
  D. bookshelf

_____ 2. Where is the gift kept?
  A. cellar
  B. barn
  C. pantry
  D. attic

_____ 3. What is Mrs. Phillips' travel destination?
  A. England
  B. Arizona
  C. Italy
  D. South Pacific

_____ 4. What is the name of the Silver Knight?
  A. Sir James
  B. King Arthur
  C. Sir Simon
  D. King Charles

_____ 5. What brings the Silver Knight to life?
  A. Alastor's touch
  B. Lady Elinore's touch
  C. William's touch
  D. Calendar's touch

_____ 6. What does Mr. Lawrence make for the castle?
  A. moat
  B. drawbridge
  C. portcullis
  D. tower

_____ 7. In what individual sport does William participate?
A. pole vaulting
B. broad jump
C. shot put
D. gymnastics

_____ 8. How does William delay Mrs. Phillips' departure?
A. He hides her tickets.
B. He shrinks her.
C. He locks her up.
D. He gets sick.

_____ 9. Who becomes Sir Simon's first companion in the castle?
A. Alastor
B. Tolliver
C. Brian
D. Mrs. Phillips

_____ 10. Who shrinks William?
A. Alastor
B. Calendar
C. Sir Simon
D. Mrs. Phillips

_____ 11. What must William find to set himself and Mrs. Phillips free?
A. the other half of the token
B. the knight's horse
C. Alastor's dragon
D. the wizard

_____ 12. Sir Simon must train William to take on what role at the castle?
A. knight
B. wizard
C. king
D. squire

_____13. Who teaches William the rules of chivalry?
A. his mother and father
B. Sir Simon and Mrs. Phillips
C. Tolliver and Brian
D. Calendar and Alastor

_____14. What does Mrs. Phillips make to record William's adventure?
A. painting
B. firescreen
C. sculpture
D. video

_____15. Who tells William the secret of defeating the wizard?
A. Calendar
B. Alastor
C. Brian
D. Tolliver

_____16. What must William face that nobody has yet escaped?
A. dragon
B. wizard
C. mirror
D. Calendar

_____17. What does William see in the mirror?
A. mountains and rivers
B. dragons and knights
C. Sir Simon and Alastor
D. himself and Mrs. Phillips

_____18. Where is Mrs. Phillips going to put the lead wizard at the end of the story?
A. in the castle
B. in the Atlantic Ocean
C. in her bureau drawer
D. in a vault in England

Answer Key

Study Questions—Answers

Chapters 1–5 (Pages 3-48)

1. The items are Mrs. Phillips' most prized possessions. 2. William hides the keepsakes in an attempt to keep Mrs. Phillips with his family. 3. Opinion—answers will vary. 4. Opinion—answers will vary. 5. Opinion—answers will vary. 6. The surprise is an enormous stone and wooden castle which had been Mrs. Phillips' when she was a child. 7. Long ago, the knight was thrown out of his kingdom by an enemy. The legend has it that the knight will one day come back to life and reclaim his land. 8. Mrs. Phillips is returning to England to be with her brother. Mrs. Phillips also believes that William will be closer to his own parents when she leaves. 9. Bear is William's stuffed animal. 10. William gets a feeling of protection and safety with Bear along. 11. The knight is soft, warm and alive. That amazes and frightens William. 12. William learns that the Silver Knight is about the size of his index finger, is a soldier, is puzzled and curious about William, acts human, and talks of magic, tokens and spells. 13. Opinion—answers will vary. 14. William was the shortest kid in class and Jason wore thick glasses. They were usually the brunt of everybody's jokes. Being together helped them develop tough skins and deaf ears. 15. William is concerned about the Silver Knight. He wants to keep the knight hidden. 16. The wizard, Alastor, supplanted Sir Simon in the kingdom. Alastor turned the knight into lead and made him very small. He did not remember anything until William touches him. 17. Sir Simon wants to test the medal. 18. Janus is a Roman mythological god having two faces. The faces of Janus are the parts of the medal.

Chapters 6–9 (Pages 49-92)

19. He proclaims electricity and electric lights to be a miracle. 20. He makes a reasonable guess. 21. Opinion—answers will vary. 22. Mr. Lawrence likes the castle. 23. Mr. Lawrence decides to build a moat for the castle. 24. Sir Simon reduces the size of the mouse. He then kills it, and prepares it for cooking. He later cooks and eats the mouse. 25. William brings Sir Simon water in a small mustard jar, and a toothpaste cap for scooping the water out. 26. Opinion—answers will vary. 27. William thinks Mrs. Phillips would be the right lady for Sir Simon. He plans to shrink her. 28. William shrinks Mrs. Phillips as she is walking to the bus. 29. William doesn't want to face Mrs. Phillips. He did not get her permission before he shrank her. 30. Mrs. Phillips refuses to speak to William until he returns her to her proper size. 31. Mr. Lawrence comes home early. He proposes that he and William try different recipes for the new wok that Mr. Lawrence purchased. 32. William accepts his father as he is. William reminds his father of promises and expectations. 33. Mrs. Phillips wants William to be small too. 34. Opinion—answers will vary. 35. Opinion—answers will vary. 36. William decides to have Sir Simon shrink him.

Chapters 10–13 (Pages 93-139)

37. The castle is very well-equipped. 38. Sir Simon tells William the rules of chivalry. Mrs. Phillips adds, "Be ever loyal in love" (page 98). 39. In the morning, Sir Simon teaches William how to use his weapons, and how to be of assistance to the knight. In the afternoon, William and Mrs. Phillips play chess and backgammon. William also practices his gymnastic routines and plays his recorder. 40. Opinion—answers will vary. 41. Mrs. Phillips believes William will need his brain, his footwork, and the sense of space he has developed as a gymnast. 42. He believes in himself, and that he will have the necessary strength for whatever happens.

---

43. Opinion—answers will vary. 44. Opinion—answers will vary. 45. The "strange apparitions" seen by William and Sir Simon are mirages which could lead them off the path. They include light, silver water, and the horse, Moonlight. 46. A young boy greets William. 47. Opinion—answers will vary. 48. The birds distract William, so that he does not bite into the apple. 49. William is given food, and is told how to defeat the dragon at the castle. 50. The villagers act with curiosity. They advise William to turn back from the castle. 51. He decides to face the dragon in the morning. Remember that a knight's greatest strength is said to be in the morning. 52. The music soothes William's nerves, and helps him focus as he follows the advice given to him about defeating the dragon.

Chapters 14–17 (Pages 140-179)
53. The stairs lead to Alastor. 54. The routine is successful in that the wizard approves of it. However, William's dagger falls out on the floor and is picked up by Calendar. 55. Calendar sniffs the dagger and declares, "no blood." 56. One of the soldiers says that William had been directed to a side entrance away from the dragon. 57. The wizard's pets are the people of the village turned into lead statues. 58. William sees the Silver Knight and the apple-tree man's son turned into lead. 59. Opinion—answers will vary. 60. William distracts the wizard with his routine, uses the front somersault to knock the wizard to the ground, grabs the necklace and moves away. William faces the mirror and sees only himself and Mrs. Phillips. The wizard sees the locust, and is terrified. 61. William sees so little in the mirror because he is kind and gentle of spirit. 62. Calendar grabs the necklace from William's hand and turns the wizard into lead and shrinks him. She also sends him away. 63. William destroys the mirror so that no one else will have such power again. 64. William hugs Sir Simon. 65. William touches each one. 66. Sir Simon tells Calendar, "You will stay with me and live out your life in comfort, surrounded by your friends" (page 163). 67. William needs the token to restore Mrs. Phillips to her normal size. 68. William takes the lead medal off the ribbon and gives it to Sir Simon. 69. Mrs. Phillips shows the lead wizard to William. It has been sent to the castle. Mrs. Phillips takes it with her. She will drop the wizard into the Atlantic on her way to England. William may not touch the wizard, or life will be restored to him. 70. Mrs. Phillips takes the fire screen with her as a memento of the adventures. 71. Mrs. Phillips plans to drop the medallion into the Atlantic with the lead wizard.

Activity Answers

Activity #1: Knowledge Check
1 - True
2 - True
3 - False (motte = mound)
4 - True
5 - False (inside the bailey)
6 - True
7 - False (drawbridge)
8 - False (portcullis)
9 - True
10 - True

Activity #2: Castle Kriss Kross—See page 43 of this guide.

Activity #3: Scrambled Words
1. allure - e - wall walk
2. garbled - b - mixed-up
3. chivalry - d - gallantry
4. mystified - c - bewildered
5. armory - g - arsenal
6. reckoned - h - dealt
7. secretive - f - uncommunicative
8. buttery - a - pantry

Activity #4: Vocabulary—Synonym or Antonym?
1. secretive
2. deteriorating
3. resigned
4. inevitable
5. mystified
6. hasty
7. distracted
8. desperately
9. meddle
10. lame
11. rummaged
12. squeamish

Activity #5: Word Find—See page 43 of this guide.

Activity #6: Vocabulary, Definitions
1. unobstructed
2. distracted
3. lame
4. intricate
5. armory
6. allotted
7. legacy
8. quest
9. contraption
10. sheepishly

Activity #7: REBUS
1. armory
2. wardrobe
3. buttery
4. drawbridge
5. scullery

Activity #8: Word Maps—Student Generated

Activity #9: Vocabulary Word Search—See page 44 of this guide.

Activity #10: Vocabulary

1. M Y S T I F I E D
   40   14 18 17 43

2. B O O T Y
 31 33

3. P O R T C U L L I S
  9   24 13 16 41

4. C R O N E
   45

5. S C U L L E R Y
25 22 3 6 7 11 32

6. U N O B S T R U C T E D
34 39 27   19

7. G N A W E D
 15 10   8

8. F A L T E R
28   26 46

9. C H I V A L R Y
30 5 23 12 36 1

10. W I T H E R E D
29 38 44 37   47

11. W A R D R O B E
 4 35 42 2 20 21

"Y O U W I L L D O W E L L I N L I F E B E C A U S E O F
 1 2 3 4 5 6 7 8 9 10 11 12 13 14 15 16 17 18 19 20 21 22 23 24 25 26 27 28
W H O Y O U A R E I N S I D E H E R E"
29 30 31 32 33 34 35 36 37 38 39 40 41 42 43 44 45 46 47

Activity #11: Vocabulary Crossword Puzzle—See page 44 of this guide.

Activity #12: Vocabulary—Acronyms, Student Generated

Activity #13: Vocabulary—Synonym Chains, Student Generated

Activity #14: Vocabulary Review—Alphapat, Student Generated

Activity #15: Vocabulary Review

1. Q U E S T
    19   3

2. R A U C O U S
  12 13 38   22   27

3. F A L T E R
  43 33

4. C O O P E D
    30 31

5. F I R E S C R E E N
  11   14

6. D R A F T Y
  21 39 26   36

7. W I L Y
  4   16 17

8. E E R I E
  41 5 6   9

9. B A T T L E M E N T S
   1 7 20 42   32   34 25 40

10. B O O T Y
  18 37 24 29 35

A N S W E R T H E M F R A N K L Y
1 2 3 4 5 6   7 8 9 10 11 12 13 14 15 16 17

B U T D O N O T A S K T O O M A N Y Y O U R S E L F
18 19 20 21 22   23 24 25 26 27 28 29 30 31   32 33 34 35   36 37 38 39 40 41 42 43

Activity #16: Cryptogram—See page 44 of this guide.

Activity #17: Story Review

1 = A	6 = U	11 = L
2 = E	7 = H	12 = O
3 = R	8 = S	13 = M
4 = V	9 = I	14 = F
5 = C	10 = Y	15 = T

A L L Y O U H A V E T O F A C E I S T H E M I R R O R
1 11 11 10 12 6 7 1 4 2 15 12 14 1 5 2 9 8 15 7 2 13 9 3 3 12 3

Activity #18: Story Review Crossword Puzzle—See page 44 of this guide.

Activity #19: Similes—Student Generated Activity

Activity #20: Quatrain Poetry—Student Generated Activity

True—False Comprehension Quiz

1 - T	6 - T	11 - T
2 - F (Mrs. Phillips)	7 - T	12 - F (William)
3 - T	8 - F (William)	13 - T
4 - T	9 - T	14 - F (Moonlight)
5 - F (architect)	10 - F (moat)	15 - T

Short Answer Comprehension Quiz—Advanced

1. William hides Mrs. Phillips's keepsakes to keep her from leaving.
2. Mrs. Phillips gives William the castle in the attic.
3. Sir Simon of Hargrave is the Silver Knight.
4. William touches the knight to bring it to life.
5. Mr. Lawrence makes a moat for the castle.
6. William shrinks Mrs. Phillips.
7. William has Sir Simon shrink him by using the medallion.
8. William wants to help Mrs. Phillips return to normal size and to help Sir Simon.
9. William is taught the rules of chivalry by Sir Simon and Mrs. Phillips.
10. William trains with Sir Simon and does gymnastics with Mrs. Phillips.
11. Sir Simon is lured off the path by an apparition of Moonlight, his horse.
12. William gets an apple off the top of the tree for the old man.
13. The old man tells William how to defeat the dragon that guards Alastor's castle.
14. William decides to face the dragon in the morning.
15. The music soothes William's heart and makes the dragon hold its fire.

Novel Test: Identification By Clues

1 - h (William)	6 - e (Robert)
2 - c (Mr. Lawrence)	7 - i (Jason)
3 - j (Mrs. Lawrence)	8 - d (Alastor)
4 - g (Sir Simon)	9 - f (Tolliver)
5 - a (Calendar)	10 - b (Brian)

Novel Test—Advanced: Identification By Quotation

1. f (William)	6. e (Robert)
2. j (Mrs. Phillips)	7. c (Alastor)
3. a (Sir Simon)	8. i (Calendar)
4. h (Jason)	9. d (Mrs. Lawrence)
5. b (Mr. Lawrence)	10. g (Brian)

Novel Test: Fill-Ins

1. William	10. William	19. dragon
2. castle	11. chivalry	20. Alastor's
3. nanny	12. riddle	21. fool
4. England	13. Alastor	22. Calendar
5. knight	14. Sir Simon	23. mirror
6. Silver	15. Moonlight	24. himself
7. touching	16. William	25. Mrs. Phillips
8. Mrs. Phillips	17. old	26. Calendar
9. Simon	18. apple	

Novel Test—Advanced: Written Response—Student Generated

Novel Test: Multiple Choice

1 - B - castle
2 - D - attic
3 - A - England
4 - C - Sir Simon
5 - C - William's touch
6 - A - moat
7 - D - gymnastics
8 - B - He shrinks her.
9 - D - Mrs. Phillips

10 - C - Sir Simon
11 - A - the other half of the token
12 - D - squire
13 - B - Sir Simon and Mrs. Phillips
14 - B - firescreen
15 - A - Calendar
16 - C - mirror
17 - D - himself and Mrs. Phillips
18 - B - in the Atlantic Ocean

Puzzle Answers

Activity #2: Castle Kriss Kross

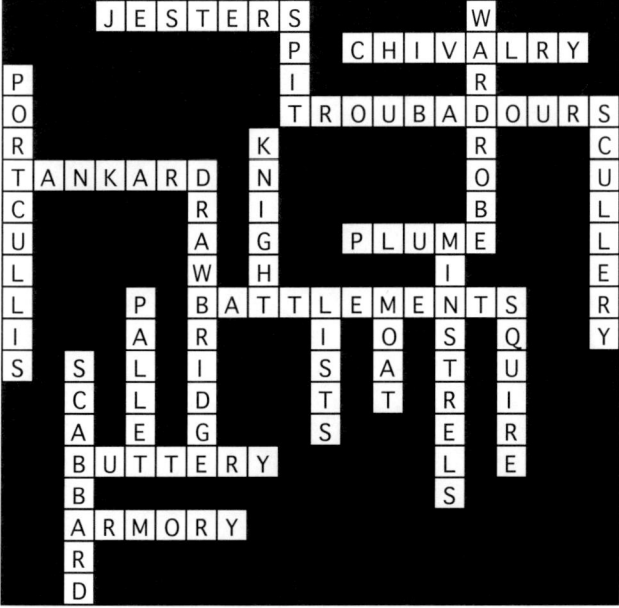

Activity #5: Word Find

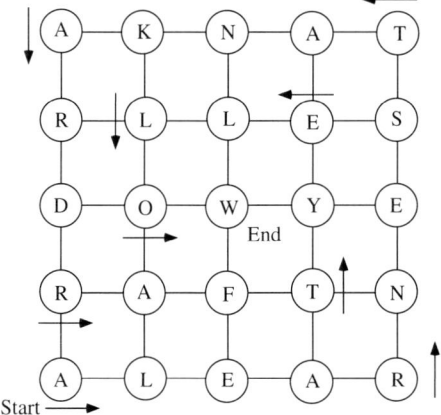

Activity #9: Vocabulary Word Search

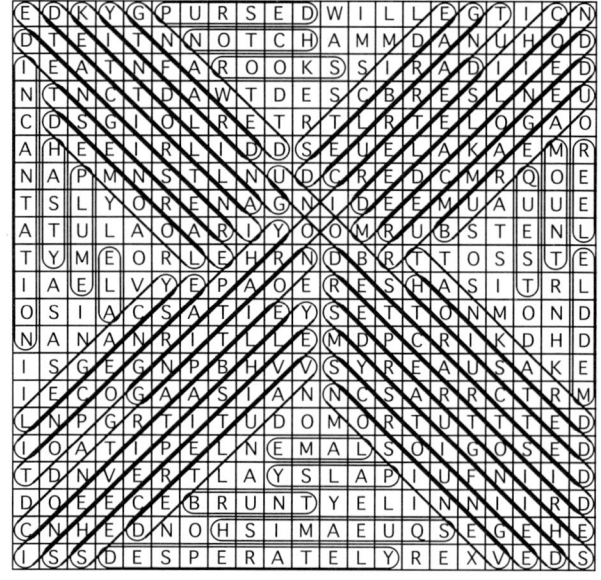

Message:
WILLIAM MUST DESTROY ALASTOR TO SAVE
SIR SIMON AND HIS KINGDOM AND LADY
ELINORE X (X = period)

Activity #11: Vocabulary Crossword Puzzle

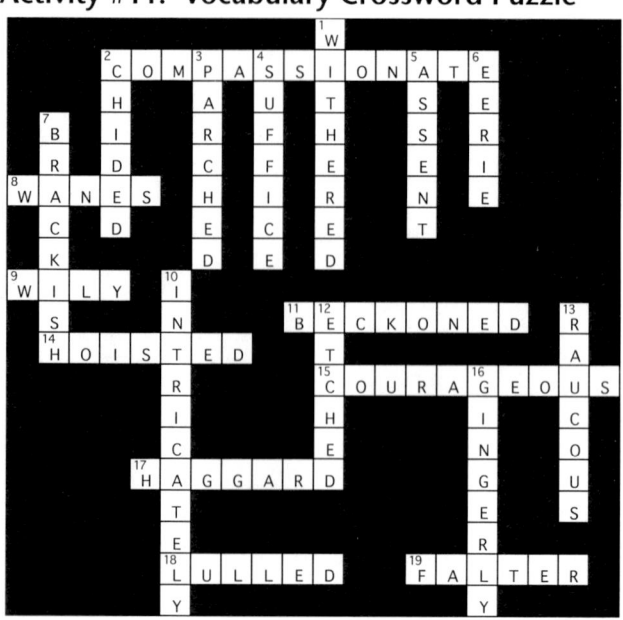

Activity #16: Cryptogram

"OTHER   PEOPLE'S   AGONIES   ARE   THE   ONLY
"TOADQ   SDTSWD P   HBTUZDP   HQD   OAD   TUWJ

PLEASURE   ALASTOR   TAKES   FROM   LIFE ."
SWDHPNQD   HWHPOTQ   OHXDP   CQTV   WZCD ."

Activity #18: Story Review Crossword Puzzle

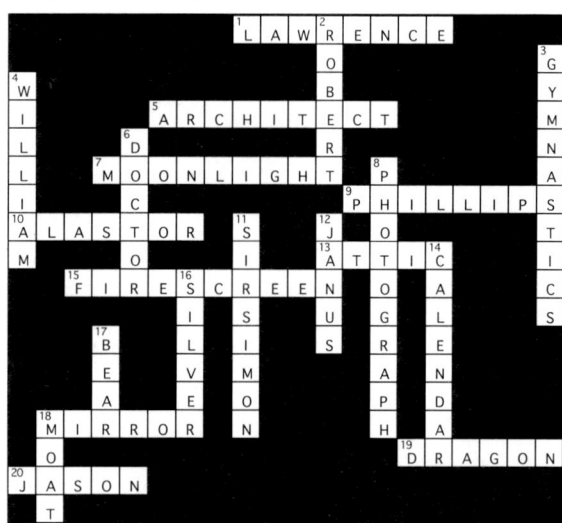